The century
in Times
Square

THE CENTURY IN TIMES SQUARE

ISBN 0-9668659-1-X
Manufactured in the United States of America
Second printing 1999

THE CENTURY IN TIMES SQUARE

Editor: Nancy Lee
Picture editor: Beth Flynn
Text editor: Merrill Perlman
Designer: Barbara Chilenskas of Bishop Books
Essay: Clyde Haberman
Chapter introductions: James Barron and Bill Harris
Captions: Bill Harris
Picture researcher: Kirsten Wilson
Text researcher: Jeff Roth
Production Editor: Jim Mones

SPECIAL THANKS TO: Linda Amster, Laura
Billingsley, Morin Bishop, Tom Burke, Tom Carley, Lisa
Carparelli, Andrea Cautela, Susan Chapple, Hugo
Colasante, Barbara Cox, Susan Dryfoos, David W. Dunlap,
Nancy Furgatch, Howard Greenberg, Pam Gubitosi, Paul
Hacker, John Hammond, Chris Joyce, Dennis Laurie,
Stuart Lavietes, Mike Levitas, Bert Lightbourne, Barbara
Mancuso, Alyse Myers, Stephanie Rice, Lee Riffaterre,
Sam Roberts, Janet Robinson, Claire Spiezio, Arthur
Sulzberger Jr., Lynne Walker

The Century in Times Square was prepared by
Bishop Books, Inc.
611 Broadway
New York, N.Y. 10012

10 9 8 7 6 5 4 3 2

ON THE COVER: Which Way Is Paris?, 1908

On Feb. 12, 1908, six automobiles left Times Square for a 20,000-mile race to Paris sponsored by The New York Times. Two army officers were handling the German entry and an Italian nobleman was behind the wheel of his country's car. The others, one American and three French, were driven by crews of professional "autoists." The route was established in three stages, with cars to be shipped by steamer from San Francisco to Seattle, then driven through Alaska and across the Bering Strait to Siberia for a home run toward Paris. They all knew there was trouble ahead when it took the lead car three days to get as far as Albany through a blinding snowstorm. Ahead were more snowdrifts, lots of mud, sandstorms, quicksand, breakdowns, wild animals and road conditions that sometimes forced drivers to use railroad rights-of-way. One of the French cars was attacked and looted by local residents in Indiana, which, according to the official protest, allowed the American car to reach San Francisco first, having driven 41 days, 8 hours and 15 minutes. Pushing on, the Americans made it through Alaska as far as Valdez before declaring the route impassable and turning back. The contestants agreed to an alternate route by steamer to Vladivostok, and gave a 30-day advantage to the American car for its Alaskan adventure. By that point, all the cars except the American, German and Italian entries had dropped out of the race. The Germans reached Paris first on July 25, followed six days later by the Americans, 170 days out of Times Square. Their 30-day advantage earned them the trophy, but they would have claimed the honor even without it. The German car, it turned out, had been shipped by train from Ogden, Utah, to Seattle, saving 1,100 miles of hard driving but adding a 30-day penalty. The Italian entry, a Brixia-Zust, limped into Paris on Sept. 17.

—*Photograph from Brown Brothers*

TITLE PAGES

Building the New Times Square, 1996

New York will be a wonderful place, people say, if it ever gets built. Others say it's wonderful already and some of them grumbled when Times Square began its makeover. But now that as much as $4 billion has been spent creating the "new" Times Square, even die-hard New Yorkers are cheering. As with other transformed neighborhoods, many will have a hard time remembering what was there before.

—*Photograph by Librado Romero/The New York Times*

Almost Halfway Into the Fifties, 1955

The Times Square New Year's Eve party welcoming 1955 was the 50th anniversary of the first celebration at 1 Times Square.

—*Photograph by Larry C. Morris/The New York Times*

Table of Contents

The Crossroads

By Clyde Haberman

Merely mentioning the name conjures a kaleidoscope of images:

Times Square.

It is rivers of neon and seas of tourists. It is sidewalk hustlers and curbside holy men. Depending on your age and where you're coming from, physically and meta-physically, it may mean a street hooker or a Virgin megastore, smoke from a Camel sign or steam from a Cup Noodles ad, New Year's Eve with Guy Lombardo or with Dick Clark, a Broadway tout or Mickey Mouse, legitimate theaters or illegitimate sex parlors, a state-of-the-art Jumbotron or an old-fashioned news ribbon over-head, 42nd Street with "The Lion King" indoors or with a three-card monte lyin' king outdoors.

Through the decades, Times Square has been exotic, erotic, neurotic and some-times just plain idiotic. But the one thing Times Square has never been, not once in all the years, is dull.

New Yorkers insist on calling it the Crossroads of the World. Of course, New Yorkers like to think of their city as the center of the cosmos, so it is hardly surpris-ing that they attach mere global import to the dot on the hometown map where Broadway and 42nd Street collide. For once, however, the New York penchant for overstatement happens to be fact.

Piccadilly Circus in London may make some think of faded empire. Piazza Venezia in Rome has vastness. L'Etoile in Paris evokes Gitanes, fedoras and Bogie driving Ingrid Bergman past L'Arc de Triomphe.

But Times Square is, without a doubt, the most recognized intersection on the planet, never more so than in the final seconds of a dying year. Hundreds of thou-sands of people huddle there in the late-December cold while tens of millions more sit in front of their television sets, watching a glittering ball inch its way down the pole atop a tower called One Times Square. By now, some are willing to believe

Don't Call It Burlesque, 1942
The New York Society for the Suppression of Vice, along with Mayor Fiorello H. LaGuardia, decided to protect the public's morals by making theater owners remove the word "burlesque" from their marquees in 1937. The bawdy bump-and-grind acts continued, but were now called "follies." They were shut down completely in 1942, only to be revived by court order in 1955.
—*Photograph by Jack Manning*

First Nighters, 1939
In his 1939 review of "Skylark," the New York Times theater critic Brooks Atkinson noted that its opening at the Morosco Theater was marked by "the goings-on of a giddy opening."
He didn't think much of the play itself, but adored its star, Gertrude Lawrence. "She chases vagrant lines up and down the stage with enormous and brilliant animation," he wrote. "The collected works of William Shakespeare would turn out to be vehicles if Miss Lawrence attacked them with the gusto that possesses her now."
—*Photograph by The New York Times*

there would not be a new year, a new century, a new millennium without this communal gathering in the heart of New York.

It wasn't always like that.

At the last turn of the century, the area was a humble place called Long Acre Square. The name was changed in 1904 when The New York Times moved there from Park Row, in lower Manhattan. Strictly speaking, Times Square is where Broadway, Seventh Avenue and 42nd Street meet. But the cachet of the Times Square name attracted people to the surrounding blocks, and the square became a neighborhood.

In short order, Times Square became the heart of the city. By World War I, dozens of theaters had planted themselves there. During one Broadway season before the stock-market crash of 1929, a record 264 shows were produced in 76 theaters, including the sumptuous New Amsterdam on 42nd Street, where Flo

Ziegfeld staged his Follies. The area was home to Tin Pan Alley, vaudeville houses and posh hotels. It was where New Yorkers by the thousands gathered for news, like updates on the 1919 World Series (though it wasn't until later that they really learned the score: the Series was fixed).

For decades to come, Times Square would provide the country with some of its more enduring images, from the finger-snap pace of the crowds outside Jack Dempsey's restaurant to the strangers exultantly embracing on V-E Day. All it took was an overhead shot of the neon-bathed square to tell moviegoers that they were entering a world of sophistication, perhaps even intrigue, far removed from their own lives. They could imagine themselves dancing at the Astor Hotel, with its triumphal arches and fountains, or walking beneath the curlicue canopy of the Paramount Theater, temple of the bobbysoxers. No matter how distant, they knew of Lindy's and its

Times Square's Quiet Hours, 1970

"In the long, lonely hours of early morning, Times Square changes," wrote McCandlish Phillips. "It ceases for a while to play its practiced role as glamor girl of the Western World." Predawn visitors, including these two sailors and their dates, "see it in what amounts to its cold cream and curlers." At 3:10 A.M, "All eight stools are occupied in a tiny eatery on 43d Street. 'Give me a bagel with a schmeer,' a night worker says and he gets it with cream cheese … 'I only got a half hour,' he says. 'I got all night,' the counterman replies." —*Photograph by Librado Romero/ The New York Times*

A Kiss Is Still a Kiss, 1999

One of the most famous photographs ever taken in Times Square is Alfred Eisenstadt's image of a sailor and a nurse kissing during a celebration of Japan's surrender and the end of World War II. Much has changed since that evening in 1945 but more than half a century later, couples still find a Times Square kiss a romantic idea, often at times when there's nothing more to celebrate than each other. Even Bugs Bunny has gotten the bug. The Old Gray Hare is one of the big stars at the never-ending show that has come to the ground floor of the former Times Tower, now called One Times Square, and home to the Warner Brothers Studio Store.
—Photograph by Librado Romero/
The New York Times

cheesecake, not to mention the Latin Quarter and its different kind of cheesecake.

With the Great Depression, Times Square started to hit the skids, slowly at first, then with a rush. By the 1970's, it had become synonymous with sleazy arcades and tawdry sex shows, a dangerous place best avoided at all costs. The menace and sheer creepiness of the place, almost a vision of hell, was memorably captured by Martin Scorsese in his 1976 film, "Taxi Driver." As for architecture, history found itself brusquely shoved aside. The Paramount Theater was sacrificed for office space, while the Astor Hotel gave way in the 1960's to a 52-story corporate filing cabinet called One Astor Plaza. The Times moved around the corner and the terra cotta facade of the old building was replaced with faceless white marble.

Every few years, civic leaders would scream that something had to be done, and they would haul out one more new plan to scrub the area clean. But nothing ever came of it. The slide seemed irreversible.

Until, almost by miracle, a real-estate boom in the 90's remade the face of

Times Square. Sex shops were swept out, and Disney and Warner Brothers stormed in. With jewel-like fidelity (and a low-interest government loan), Disney restored the long-abandoned New Amsterdam, where mushrooms grew on the orchestra floor. In an unconscious echo of the 1919 Series, many hundreds of people filled the concrete islands of the square to catch a championship basketball game on a giant television screen overhead. As the century ended, the old Times building was being flanked by taller cousins, homes for other media empires.

Not everyone loved the sanitized newcomers. Mall-style stores were alien, even offensive, to many New Yorkers. But who was prepared to argue that dope dealers and pimps were preferable to wide-eyed tourists and baby carriages?

Through the years, Times Square has evolved and is still evolving. And yet some things never change: At the dawn of a new century, it remains the place to gather, whether to watch a televised space shot or protest a war or celebrate triumph over tyranny. It is far more than a neighborhood. It is America's town square.

Put On a Happy Face, 1996
The world's first taxicabs appeared in New York in 1907 for the opening of the Plaza Hotel, when the entrepreneur Harry Allen brought out cars equipped with a device he called a "taximeter." It not only gave passengers a running tally of what the ride was costing, but put a new word, "taxi-cab," into the language. In 1937, responding to racketeering and labor problems in the cab business, Mayor Fiorello H. LaGuardia signed the Haas Act, requiring a $10 medallion to make a taxi legal, and limiting the number to 13,566. The number was reduced to about 11,000 by the 1960's, and is back up to about 12,000, but because of its limitation, the average price of a medallion has gone up to about $225,000.
—*Photograph by Linda Rosier*

NAZIS GIVE UP
SURRENDER TO ALLIES
AND RUSSIA ANNOUNCED

New York World-Telegram

IN THE NEWS

In the News

Feeling Feverish, 1963
Feeling Feverish, 1963
Firefighters from neighborhood stations are among Times Square's most frequent visitors. About 2,000 men were on the job at the turn of the last century. Today, more than 11,000 paid professionals, both men and women, work in the system that replaced volunteers in 1865. Major conflagrations are rare in Times Square, but on this October day, an advertising sign on Broadway at 43rd Street went up in smoke. The ad, for St. Joseph Aspirin, touted a quick fix for burning fevers.
—*Photograph by Carl T. Gossett Jr./*
The New York Times

It's Over Over There (Almost), 1945
(Overleaf)
On May 7, 1945, Times Square went wild when word leaked out that Germany might have surrendered, even though the official announcement was still a day away and war was still raging in the Pacific. But Mayor Fiorello H. LaGuardia was not in a celebrating mood. "I want all the people who have thoughtlessly left their jobs to return to their jobs." he shouted through loud-speakers, "and not to do it again." He also complained about the waste of valuable paper being tossed from windows. Even so, the celebration lasted seven hours.
—*Hans Knopf–Pix Inc./*
Time Inc. Picture Collection

It is where ABC-TV says "Good Morning, America" every day, where Condé Nast's slick and stylish magazines are prepared and where Reuters' no-nonsense headline-every-minute wire-service reports soon will be. Times Square is the perfect home for news-gatherers and communications companies like Viacom, with its MTV studios overlooking Broadway, and Bertelsmann, the German conglomerate with its RCA recording label and Doubleday book subsidiary. And it is where The New York Times has made the news fit to print since 1904.

But if a lot of news comes *from* Times Square, a lot of it is made *in* Times Square, too. For Times Square is the perfect listening post. It is New York's village green, a round-the-clock gathering-place where New Yorkers attempt to explain what they are thinking and why, what they are doing and why, what they are eating and why, what they like and why, what they dislike — you get the idea. No wonder the world watches the watchers in Times Square, and not just when the clock strikes 12 and the crowd bursts into "Auld Lang Syne" every Dec. 31. Wars, elections, the stock market's ups and downs, natural disasters a world away, the headline that seems so important today but is sure to be forgotten by tomorrow — in Times Square, everybody has something to say about it. Something eloquent, poignant and quotable.

One reason is numbers: concerts and demonstrations in Times Square draw more people than the population of Jackson, Wyo., and something always seems to be happening there. In Times Square, Andy Warhol's 15 minutes are just not long enough.

The Place to Be, 1938

Before the ball was lowered down the Times Building's flagpole to welcome 1938, some were saying that nobody would show up to watch. In 1937, Americans spent $900 million for radios and they were staying home to listen to Edgar Bergen, Kate Smith and Rudy Vallee. But the predictions were wrong. Even the streetcars came to a standstill as crowds mobbed the square to welcome another new year.

—*Photograph by Times Wide World Photos*

The Year in Lights, 1978

At the end of 1978, about a century after Thomas Edison invented the electric light, technicians were impressed by how much the old Times Square tradition of New Year's Eve ball-lowering had been improved. This version, which had halogen lamps for higher visibility, replaced a six-foot ball that had ordinary light bulbs. The ball manufactured to mark the Year 2000 was designed and made by Waterford Crystal. It features 144 glitter strobe lights, a 10,000-watt internal xenon lamp and an aluminum skin covered with 12,000 large rhinestones. The lowering, which takes one minute, is down a 77-foot flagpole on top of One Times Square.

—*Photograph by Chester Higgins Jr./ The New York Times*

Come Blow Your Horn, 1969

The Times moved most operations from its tower in 1913, but kept the New Year's Eve tradition it started until it sold the building in 1961 to Douglas Leigh, the man who brought animated billboards (he called them "Spectaculars") to Times Square. Leigh renamed the tower for the Allied Chemical Company, his major tenant, and remodeled it with a sleek marble exterior, a single sign at the top and a redesigned news "zipper" run for a time by LIFE Magazine. Leigh continued dropping lighted balls to welcome each new year.

—Photograph by Librado Romero/ The New York Times

A Hero's Welcome, 1951

President Harry S. Truman dismissed Gen. Douglas MacArthur as General of the Army on April 11, 1951, in a dispute over the Korean War. The general came home to address Congress and bask in the acclaim of those who disagreed with Truman's action, or at least remembered MacArthur's triumphs in World War II. When he arrived in New York on April 20, he was driven through Central Park, then down Broadway through Times Square, where he was showered with affection and confetti. He was whisked down to the Battery, where 10,000 marchers, including veterans' groups and military bands, were waiting to join him in a ticker tape parade up to City Hall. He told Grover Whalen, the city's official greeter, "I have traveled 10,000 miles in the last eight days to find out who truly rules in the United States."

—Photograph by Carl T. Gossett Jr./ The New York Times

The Army of the Unemployed, 1930
Before the Great Depression that followed the 1929 Wall Street crash, being out of work had been considered vaguely shameful. But in the 30's there were too many jobless people to ignore and it became acceptable for them to demonstrate with dignity, as these men did. They marched through Times Square wearing signs that identified their occupation and their offer to work for a dollar a week.
  —*Photograph by The Associated Press*

Light at the End of the Tunnel, 1936
After becoming President in 1933, Franklin D. Roosevelt began a series of ambitious programs to deal with the Depression, including Social Security, public works and wage-and-hour laws. Among the programs, Boulder Dam was finished just in time for the 1936 election, and the flood of voters to the polls was overwhelming. Roosevelt beat his opponent, Alf Landon, by almost two votes to one. Though there may have been little suspense, it didn't stop crowds from gathering to follow minute-by-minute election night coverage.
  —*Photograph by Times Wide World Photos*

"Hell No, I Won't Go," 1965

The Armed Forces recruiting booth in Times Square, the most active in the country, was a focal point of protests against United States policy in Southeast Asia during the 1960's. This protest, at a time when the number of Americans fighting in Vietnam increased from 22,000 to about 184,000, became a melee when a critic of the demonstration chimed in with a difference of opinion. The recruiting station itself, built on the traffic island at 43rd Street in the 1950's, was torn down in 1999 and replaced by what recruiters are calling a "state-of-the-art" facility. (Translation: it has a rest room, something the builders of the original neglected to include.) —*Photograph by Patrick A. Burns/The New York Times*

Remembering King, 1968
On April 5, the day Dr. Martin Luther King Jr. was assassinated in Memphis, deep anger led to rioting throughout the country. In New York, except for a few demonstrations, like this one, the mood was more one of sorrow. At about midnight, a group began a vigil that lasted until morning. One mourner described it as "a spontaneous thing. One friend called another."
—*Photograph by William E. Sauro/The New York Times*

Catching the World Series, 1919
King Albert I and Queen Elizabeth of Belgium arrived in New York on Oct. 2, 1919, but in Times Square all eyes were glued to the Times Building for play-by-play bulletins of the World Series game in Cincinnati. The Reds beat the Chicago White Sox 9-1 that day and went on to win the Series, five games to three. The Times reported that the first game was "so one-sided that the heralded White Sox looked like bush leaguers." Did the Sox throw the game? Months later, more crowds gathered in Times Square for up-to-the-minute reports that the team they were now calling "the Black Sox" probably did.
—*Photograph by Paul Thompson*

Have You Heard? The War's Over, 1945
New Year's Eve celebrations notwithstanding, one of the biggest crowds gathered in
Times Square on Aug. 14, 1945, to celebrate the end of the war with Japan. The Times
news "zipper" went dark at 7 o'clock that evening and then after a few seconds, the
lights flashed on again. "***OFFICIAL*** TRUMAN ANNOUNCES JAPANESE
SURRENDER," it said, and the roar of the crowd could be heard to the middle of Central
Park. The stars in the headline were a tribute to the three branches of the armed forces:
the Army, Navy and Marine Corps (the Air Corps was still part of the Army back then).
The headline itself was written by The Times's publisher, Arthur Hays Sulzberger.
—*Photograph by Patrick A. Burns/The New York Times*

Death of a Dictator, 1945
Adolf Hitler's death was reported in
newspapers on May 2, 1945. This G.I.,
with three overseas service bars on his
sleeve, knew that the odds of him earning
a fourth just became a lot slimmer.
—*Photograph by the New York Times*

Been There, Done That, 1899

Among the most famous weather events in New York's history was the Blizzard of 1888 which, as The Times put it, left the city "crushed under the snow" and completely immobile for more than two days. When nature staged an encore in '99, immobilization was kept to a minimum because work crews and police officers had experience by then. Among the few benefits of the earlier blizzard was the elimination of utility poles and the placing of telephone, telegraph and electrical wiring underground.

—Photograph from the Byron Collection/The Museum of the City of New York

The Night the Lights Went Out, 1965

During the Blizzard of 1888, the new streetlights went out for more than three hours. But it was nothing compared to the evening of Nov. 9, 1965, when all the lights went out in the Northeast — including most of New York City — after an electrical relay failed in Canada. The 13-hour blackout hit in the middle of the rush hour, leaving 800,000 trapped in subways. Traffic slowly moved through Times Square after police officers set up lights and stood at the intersections waving cars and buses on their way. History repeated itself in the city in July 1977, when lightning struck Con Ed's Indian Point nuclear generating plant.
—*Photograph by Allyn Baum/ The New York Times*

Happy Birthday Broadway, 1926

When Peter Minuit, director general of the Dutch West India Company, stepped onto Manhattan Island in 1626, Broadway was an Indian trail. It was improved in fits and starts until Heere Straat, as the Dutch called it, became a link between New Amsterdam and Fort Orange, the Dutch settlement up the Hudson that became known as Albany. During the tercentenary celebration in 1926, Times Square was the focal point of a parade that included floats, automobiles and 12 marching bands.

—*Photograph by Times Wide World Photos*

Election Night, 1960

When John F. Kennedy assumed office, he became the first president born in the 20th century. And, at 43, he was also the youngest man ever elected. (Theodore Roosevelt was actually the youngest president; he took office at 42 after the assassination of President William McKinley.) The vote in the election was very close. The Kennedy-Johnson ticket took New York State with 3,830,085 votes, compared to Nixon's 3,446,419.

—*Photograph by Robert C. Walker/The New York Times*

The Show's Over, 1967

The week it opened in November 1926, the 3,664-seat Paramount Theater set a world record at the box office, taking in $80,000. Ticket prices ranged from 40 to 75 cents, and went up to 99 cents on weekends. The first theater worthy of the name "picture palace," the Paramount replaced a long-running Times Square hit, Shanley's Restaurant, that had served the sporting crowd at Broadway and 43rd Street through most of the Gilded Age. In 1932, a run of bad movies prompted the theater's owners to add stage shows with name acts, and it became the liveliest place in town. Nothing lasts forever, though, and in 1967 wrecking crews arrived to gut the theater and replace it with office space. Television was the villain, they said.

—*Photograph by Carl T. Gossett Jr./*
The New York Times

Have a Drink on Us, 1933

When a Constitutional Amendment made it illegal to sell alcoholic beverages in 1919, New Yorkers began drinking vile potables in some 32,000 speakeasies, double the number of pre-Prohibition drinking establishments. As Mayor Jimmy Walker put it: "Prohibition is a wonderful idea. I just wonder when it's going to start." Legal restaurants served "near beer," a malt beverage of less than one-half of 1 percent alcohol, and when Prohibition was repealed in 1933, one staged a "funeral" for it.

—*Photograph from UPI/Corbis*

We're In This Together, 1942

America's entry into World War II brought a new wave of patriotism. Among those who promoted the idea that we are all Americans was Mayor Fiorello H. LaGuardia, who had been born in New York City, the son of a Sephardic Jewish mother and an Italian father, both immigrants. In 1916, he became the first Italian-American elected to Congress. And, as a reminder of his boyhood in the American West, where his father was a bandmaster in the Army, Hizzoner usually wore a 10-gallon hat.

—*Photograph by The New York Times*

Macy Day, 1937
Although it has been called
"Macy's Thanksgiving Day
Parade" since Santa Claus
first marched down
Broadway to Herald Square
in 1924, New Yorkers insist
on calling it the "Macy Day
Parade." The most exciting
leg of the march has always
been through Times Square,
where the giant balloons,
introduced in 1927, com-
pete with the signs hung
from building facades.
Pinocchio floated past
crowds with his 44-foot
nose, more than a decade
after the parade's inception.
—*Photographer Unknown*

A Windy Day, 1997

On Thanksgiving Day 1997, 43-mile-per-hour winds put many of Macy's big balloons on the disabled list. First, the Cat in the Hat hit a lamppost at 72nd Street, injuring two spectators. Barney had to be pulled out of the line of march at 51st Street and the Pink Panther crashed in the middle of Times Square. When it started to wobble ominously, a police officer rammed a knife into the big cat's tail and it settled down on the pavement on top of some of its handlers. In spite of the unexpected high drama, some two million spectators emerged unscathed and enchanted.

—*Photograph by Andrea Mohin/The New York Times*

The News In Lights, 1997

When James J. Jeffries fought Jack Johnson to reclaim boxing's heavyweight title in 1910 (and lost), The Times installed an electric bulletin board on its tower to give fans a blow-by-blow description. In 1928, just in time to see if Gotham's own Al Smith would become the next president (he didn't), The Times installed a band of light bulbs that girdled the tower and spelled out the results. The "zipper" has had many masters over the years. In its latest digitized version, which replaced the zipper being dismantled in this photo, it carries news reports from Dow Jones.

—*Photograph by Angel Franco/The New York Times*

UPTOWN
TO UPPER MANHATTA
AND THE BRONX
EXIT
DOWN THIS
STAIRWAY
TO BMT

PEOPLE IN THE SQUARE

People in the Square

Mail Call, 1946

Times Square Station, the post office on 42nd Street west of Eighth Avenue, handles almost 400,000 pieces of mail every day, not counting the volume at its satellites, the Bryant Station on 43rd Street and the station at Rockefeller Center. Back in the 1940's, outgoing mail was picked up from boxes mounted on light poles by letter carriers who loaded penny postcards and three-cent letters into canvas bags, then walked back to their base to hand-sort them. Pickups are handled by truck today, and the sorting is done electronically, a process that was made simpler in 1963 when ZIP Codes were added and Times Square acquired an alias: New York, N.Y. 10036.
—*Photograph by Arthur Brower/ The New York Times*

Stranded, 1957
(Overleaf)

At 5 in the morning on Dec. 9, 1957, subway motormen staged a wildcat strike and many of the trains came to an unexpected halt. As the day wore on, other transit unions joined the strike, although Mike Quill, the president of the Transport Workers Union who would become famous for keeping his members off the job for 12 days in 1966, refused to support this one. Through the evening rush hour, transit officials announced that two-thirds of the subways were running. The problem for people in the Times Square Station was finding out which third was not.
—*Photograph by Robert C. Walker/ The New York Times*

There is no better place to people-watch than Times Square. Razzle-dazzle vaude-villains and hipper-than-hip hip-hop performers? Freshly pressed Army recruiters and leftover draft dodgers? Confetti-hurlers and Sanitation Department cleaner-uppers? The gawking tourist and the get-out-of-my-way New Yorker? They are all here, and are easily the most fascinating thing about the place. They all consider Times Square their playground, a few square blocks where they can be themselves, if not by themselves. They know each other — maybe not by name, but by location and occupation: The hustler who steers visitors to this or that double-decker sight-seeing bus knows the dashboard-pounding cabby who waits at the hotels around the corner. The cabby knows the delivery-service driver who double-parks at the curb. The delivery-service driver knows who's who: the nail-biting producer who worries that his next show will be a flop, the investment banker who worries that London will quibble with her latest takeover proposal, the bartender at the place down the street who heads home when things quiet down around 3 in the morning. Don't look for *him* before tomorrow afternoon.

Contenders, 1993
When Madison Square Garden was just around the corner from Times Square, anyone with any dreams of making it in the boxing ring made their way to any one of a dozen local gyms specializing in the art. One of the last of them, the Times Square Gym at 1466 Broadway, still attracts hopefuls who find that health clubs and other upstart gyms just can't do the job in quite the same old-fashioned way.
—Photograph by Angel Franco/The New York Times

Soapbox, 1961
Anyone can say just about anything in New York, but preachers and other special pleaders tend to gravitate to the street corners of Times Square. It guarantees a big audience — and one that is likely to talk back.
—Photograph by John C. Orris/The New York Times

Saving Souls, 1961

Before there were shelters and rehabilitation centers, Times Square street people found help and a little old-time religion at the Salvation Army's storefront church on 49th Street west of Seventh Avenue. Damon Runyon, who lived nearby at the Hotel Forrest on Broadway, may have used this institution, or at least its predecessor, as the inspiration for the mission that was central to the stories he wrote that became another Broadway institution, the musical "Guys and Dolls."

—*Photograph by Larry C. Morris/The New York Times*

He Who Must Be Obeyed, 1948

Orchestrating the movements of aggressive drivers has been the chore of traffic cops since the invention of the car. They got some help, however, from traffic lights, which first appeared in New York in 1922 at Fifth Avenue intersections between 42nd and 59th Streets. Police officers manually switched them from red to green. The first automated traffic lights appeared two years later — in Times Square.

—*Photographer unknown*

Lunch Break, 1957

People complain that the streets of Times Square always seem to be torn up for construction. But the people doing the digging always have good reasons. Con Edison's theme in the 50's, "dig we must for a better New York," would not apply to a man's own time, and this one takes a load off his feet during a meal break.

—*Photograph by Ernie Sisto/The New York Times*

Gone Fishin', 1959

A bit of chewing gum or a dab of axle grease on a weight at the end of a piece of string were the working tools of New York's sidewalk fishermen, who found the best hauls from grates next to sidewalk newsstands. The New York Times columnist Meyer Berger once interviewed one of the pros who told him that Times Square had the best fishing holes of all. "After the early evening rush," he said, "the bus stop on the east side of the Times Building is nearly always good for 20 to 30 cents." In the summer of 1999, The Times's City section reported that sidewalk fishermen are still working the grates, except that these days they use wooden poles tipped with chewing gum rather the lengths of string. But as one of the pros pointed out, the pickings on the sidewalks are sometimes better than what's to be found under them.

—*Photograph by Allyn Baum/The New York Times*

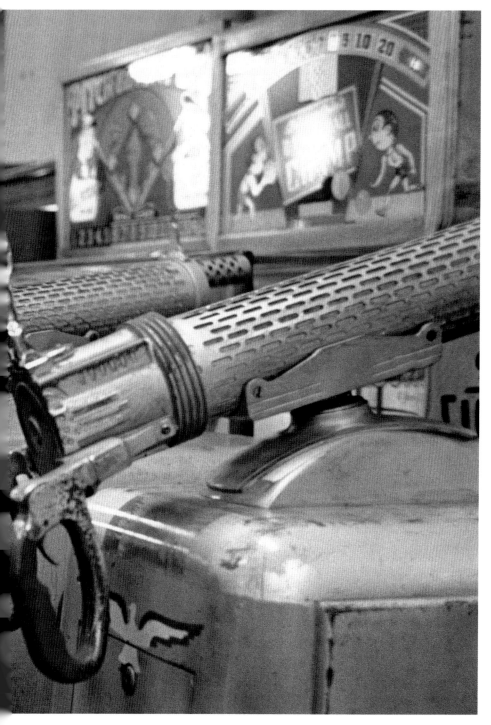

Test Your Skill, 1953

Fire a machine gun in Times Square these days and you're going to have some explaining to do. But there was a time when the only explanation you'd need was how in the world you missed that target right in front of your eyes. Along with Skee Ball and pinball and bingo, target shooting was a way to prove how skillful you were 50 years ago. You could play three-card monte back then, too, but players were hard to find — even then, everybody knew that it was no game of skill.

—*Photograph by Sam Falk/The New York Times*

Santa's Helpers, 1964

New York streets are filled every holiday season with Men in Red (these days, even with some Women in Red), collecting for those less fortunate. These Volunteers of America began their season by serenading the Queens poster child for the March of Dimes, but it would seem that the bells were not music to his ears.

—*Photograph by Arthur Brower/
The New York Times*

The Sign That Puffed, 1964

One of the most enduring images of Times Square is the Camel Man, who blew smoke rings around the clock for decades from a billboard mounted on the Claridge Hotel on Broadway between 43rd and 44th Streets. During World War II, the image switched from soldiers to sailors to airmen, but the puffing never stopped until the hotel, which served as a location for the film "Midnight Cowboy," was replaced by an office building and movie theater. The theater has recently been replaced by a studio for ABC Television's "Good Morning America."

—*Photograph by Eddie Hausner/
The New York Times*

Whaddya Read?, 1970

New York has been a newspaper town since The New York Gazette was first published in 1725. By the beginning of the 20th century, hundreds of newspapers had been published in the city in just about every language. By the time this newsstand dealer arrived for work in the summer of 1970, the number of major dailies had dropped in less than a decade from eight to four: The Post, The Daily News, The Wall Street Journal and The Times. Gone were The Daily Mirror, The Journal-American, The Herald-Tribune and The World-Telegram & Sun. But New York still has more daily papers than any other American city.

—Photograph by Librado Romero/The New York Times

Lights Out, 1946

As the song says, "when a Broadway baby says good night, it's early in the morning." In those predawn hours, most of Broadway's bright lights have been turned off and there is a strange kind of twilight in Times Square as the city that never sleeps takes a catnap.

*—Photograph by Patrick A. Burns/
The New York Times*

What's in a Name?

On April 8, 1904, Mayor George B. McClellan and the Board of Aldermen officially changed the name of Long Acre Square to Times Square in honor of The Times's new building. But every now and then in the years since, the Square is given a temporary name to honor causes, including:

1943 — "Bondway," promoting a drive to sell war bonds.
Photograph by The New York Times
1946 — "Donut Corner," honoring World War II programs to keep servicemen fat and happy. *Photographer Unknown*
1950 — "77th Division Boulevard," marking the reunion of the men in the division who fought in both world wars.
Photograph by Meyer Liebowitz/The New York Times
1951 — "Dimes Square," kicking off the March of Dimes campaign with an assist from Mayor Robert F. Wagner.
Photograph by Patrick A. Burns/The New York Times
1957 — "Civil Defense Square," generating support for cold war readiness. *Photograph by John C. Orris/The New York Times*
1964 — "Salvation Army Square," calling attention to the kettles.
Photograph by Patrick A. Burns/The New York Times
1965 — "Warsaw Ghetto Square," for the 22nd anniversary of the uprising. *Photograph by Meyer Liebowitz/The New York Times*

Get a Horse, 1959

There are 68 licensed horse-drawn carriages in New York. The law forbids them to carry passengers on city streets between the hours of 10 a.m. and 9 p.m., except at Central Park, where $34 will buy you a half-hour tour of the Drive between 59th and 72nd Streets. They are also forbidden to operate when the temperature rises above 90 degrees or goes below 18 degrees. Many horses are stabled in four-story buildings in Hell's Kitchen, west of Times Square, and regularly plod through its streets on their way to and from work.

—*Photograph by Eddie Hausner/
The New York Times*

The Last of the Red-Hot P.R. Men, 1991

When wrecking crews arrived to tear down the Longacre Building so work could go forward in the creation of the new Times Square, they had to deal with a holdout in the person of Richard R. Falk, a public relations man whose office was in the building. He had been representing would-be celebrities, Broadway shows, restaurants and nightclubs from that desk since the 1940's and he wasn't going to go quietly. The self-described "liar for hire" finally succumbed to a court order, but he went out smiling. "All my life I'm looking for space in the papers, I'm dying for it and now it's falling on me," he said. "It took me 50 years, but I made it. I'm going out in style." Falk died in 1994 at the age of 81.

—*Photograph by Fred R. Conrad/
The New York Times*

My Name's Maxie. What's Yours?, 1953
You could buy a bronzed Statue of Liberty or Empire State Building from any Times Square souvenir stand, but what could top a big floppy hat? Maxie could even stitch your name on it for you. Other tiny stores like his could sell you a newspaper with a headline you wrote yourself or a cold tropical drink served under waving palm trees.

—*Photograph by Sam Falk/The New York Times*

Box Lunch, 1954
After Jack Dempsey retired from the ring, the heavyweight boxing champion became a Times Square fixture outside his restaurant at Broadway and 49th Street. The mural that dominated the place recalled the 1919 fight against Jess Willard that gave him the title he held until 1926. Heavyweight champion Jack Sharkey, middleweight champ Mickey Walker and lightweight champ Tony Canzoneri also had restaurants in the neighborhood near the old Madison Square Garden, where their other careers flourished.

—*Photograph by Sam Falk/The New York Times*

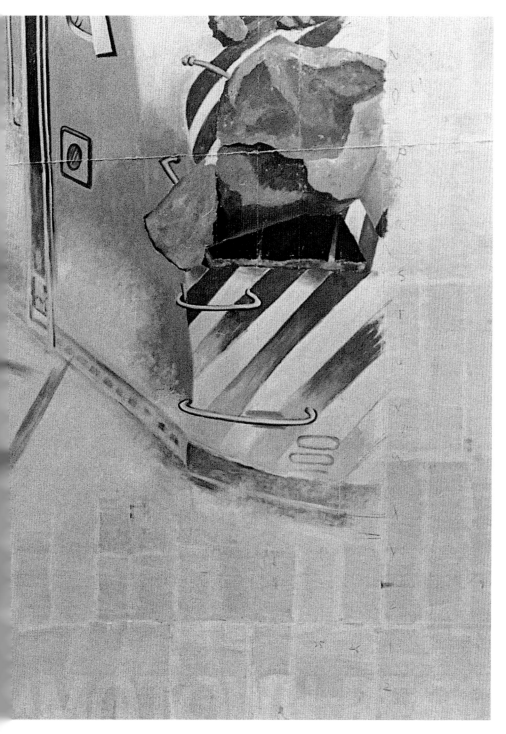

Billboard Art, 1976
Before billboards were produced on vinyl panels and unrolled at their intended sites, they were an art form created on the spot by sign painters only a few degrees removed from mural painters. Posters like this one for the movie "Silver Streak" were created as small paintings in art studios and then taken to the site, where they were divided into small squares matching a larger grid traced on the space to be filled. Then the painters reproduced the work a square at a time.
—*Photograph by D. Gorton/*
The New York Times

Dining Out at 4 a.m., 1946

If New York is the city that never sleeps, it is also the city that never seems to stop eating, especially in Times Square, where a photographer found these people snacking and schmoozing at 4 in the morning. What would you give to know what this man just said to his date? The counterman will never tell.

—*Photograph by Patrick A. Burns/The New York Times*

BEATLES PLEASE STAY HERE 4-EVER

GEORGE

JOHN

PAUL

RINGO

I LOVE GEORGE

Hero Worship, 1964
When the Beatles arrived in New York for the first time in February 1964, The Times reported: "There were girls, girls and more girls. Whistling girls. Screaming girls. Singing girls." During their visit, the Fab Four made their first live television appearance on "The Ed Sullivan Show" and staged two concerts at Carnegie Hall as well as a benefit show at the Paramount Theater which, thanks to Frank Sinatra, already had plenty of experience with screaming teenage girls.
—*Photograph by Jack Manning/The New York Times*

Sister, Can You Spare a Doughnut?, 1957

A tradition began in 1917 when Salvation Army workers shared their doughnuts with doughboys serving in France in World War I. The anniversary of the event was marked in Times Square when a pair of Salvation Army officers handed out doughnuts to passers-by. But not before teasing a G.I. whose nose was pressed to the window of the U.S.O Canteen on 43rd Street.

—*Photograph by John C. Orris/The New York Times*

Shine, Mister?, 1944

Before they called such things protecting the "quality of life," plainclothes policemen routinely went out into Times Square to sweep the streets clear of kids who blocked the sidewalks shining shoes. On this particular morning, they rounded up 35 of them, ranging in age from 8 to 14, and took them to the Times Square Information Booth, where squad cars moved them to the station house. Then their parents were called to take them home. A police officer stressed that they were not under arrest, but pointed out that if they were adults they'd be charged with a misdemeanor. The young entrepreneurs earned $2 to $3 a day, about what a single shoeshine would bring today.

—*Photograph by The New York Times*

Beating the Heat, 1996

After catching snowflakes on your nose and eyelashes, one of life's great pleasures is catching raindrops on your tongue on a steamy summer day when the sky turns black and a sudden downpour begins. New York averages 40 inches of rain a year. February, with an average of 3.13 inches, is the driest month, and March is the wettest at 4.22 inches, thanks to a clash of warm air from the south and winter's last arctic air.

—Photograph by Chang W. Lee/The New York Times

Snow Fun, 1955

New York averages about 29 inches of snow every year. But every now and then, enough of it sticks to make a sled handy on 42nd Street.

—Photograph by Arthur Brower/
The New York Times

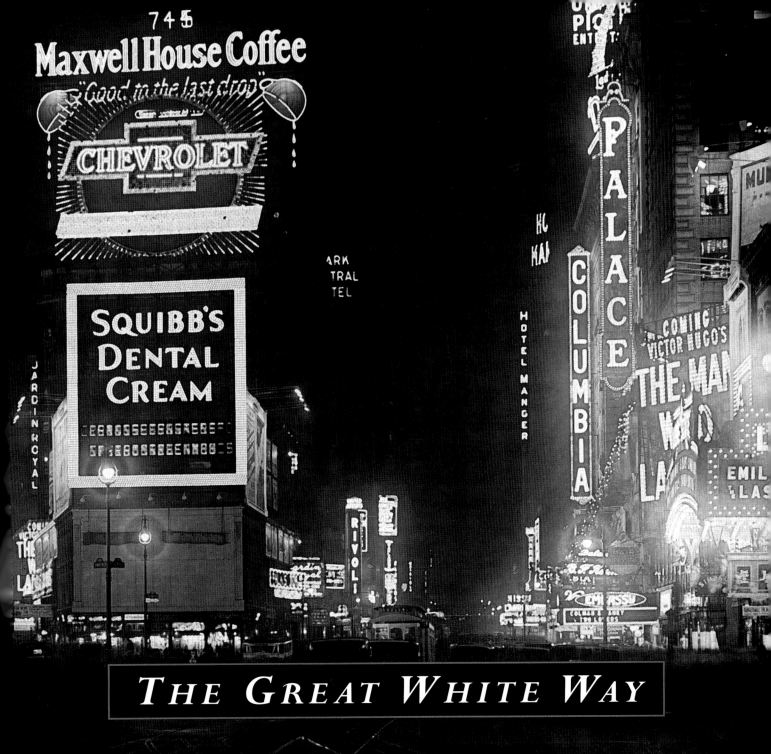

THE GREAT WHITE WAY

The Great White Way

The Iceman Cometh, 1946
Eugene O'Neill, born in Times Square at the Barrett House hotel on 43rd Street in 1888, began his career as a playwright on Cape Cod. He came back to Broadway in 1920 with a production of his Pulitzer Prize-winning "Beyond the Horizon." His play "The Iceman Cometh" was produced on Broadway in 1946, but didn't get the recognition it deserved until José Quintero staged it Off Broadway at Circle in the Square, with Jason Robards as its star, 10 years later.
—*Photograph by George Karger/ LIFE Magazine*

Lights Over Broadway, 1928
(Overleaf)
When the British novelist G.K. Chesterton first saw Times Square, he wrote, "What a garden of earthly delights this would be if only one had the gift of not being able to read."
—*Photograph from Culver Pictures*

There's no business like show business, and in show business, there's no place like Times Square. For high-kicking Ziegfeld Follies choristers and fast-writing Tin Pan Alley tunesmiths like Irving Berlin and George Gershwin, for theater legends like Ethel Barrymore and Basil Rathbone, for audition-bound newcomers dreaming of that one big break, for stage-door Johnnys who insist they want only an autograph, Times Square is where the real-life dramas are played out. Raffish Damon Runyons? Larger-than-life Broadway Danny Rose types? Times Square has room for them all beneath its glitzy, glowing thicket of neon signs and smoke-puffing billboards. For a while, it even had its own Mona Lisa, 250 times the size of the original.

Times Square got its theaters because the rest of the nation wanted a peek at New York shows. A theater owners' syndicate had been exporting shows to other cities since 1896, and they discovered that the more shows they could produce in New York, the more money they could make, at home and on the road. Thus rose the hometown stages — Beaux-Arts temples with ornate columns, mansard roofs and ceilings embellished with Tiffany glass. These turn-of-the-century theaters were also monuments to incredible profits. In the early years of the century, a big show could earn an average of a million dollars in its first year. The theater owner typically kept about 40 percent. In the final year of the century, Broadway was still packing them in, with attendance a record 11.6 million and a box-office take of $588 million, also a record.

Star Power, 1938

"You're going out a youngster," the impresario tells the chorus girl in the musical "42nd Street." "You've *got* to come back a star." But the time-honored route from the chorus to stardom was sidetracked in 1919 when the Actors Equity union shut down Broadway in a dispute involving chorus girls. They had been forced to rehearse free for a dozen weeks with no guarantee of a job if the show ever opened. The monthlong strike, which cost producers half a million a week but won rehearsal pay for the chorus girls, stopped 60 shows in rehearsal and closed 35 theaters.

—*Photograph by Eric Schaal © Time Inc.*

A Chorus Line, 1983

In 1983, when "A Chorus Line" became Broadway's longest-running hit up until that time, its 3,389th performance was a reunion of 332 dancers from present and previous casts. They came, as The Times noted, "from the four continents to which they had dispersed, from stardom and from unemployment lines." The show put on a total of 6,137 performances, a record eventually beaten by "Cats."

—*Photograph by Fred R. Conrad/The New York Times*

OOOHH, It's Him!, 1944

Police estimated the Times Square crowd at 25,000. They were all headed in the direction of the Paramount Theater, as they would for the next three weeks, and it is safe to say that few of them were going there to see the movie "Our Hearts Were Young and Gay." Frank Sinatra, "The Voice," was going to appear there. It was also when the world heard screams of bobbysoxer pleasure, a phenomenon some said had been dreamed up by Sinatra's press agent. Whether a stunt or spontaneous emotion, teenagers are still reacting in the same way outside the MTV studio just up the street.
—*Photograph by AP/Wide World Photos*

Close Quarters, 1948

In an editorial during the summer of 1999, The New York Times addressed the not-so-new problem of pedestrian gridlock in Times Square. "The real theater this fall will unfold on Broadway, the street," it predicted. Pointing to crowds under MTV's street-front studio, the arrival of ABC's "Good Morning America" and visitors lining up at the TKTS booth for low-cost theater tickets, not to mention the arrival of Condé Nast and the World Wrestling Federation, it suggested that "as entertaining as it might be to watch wrestling stars like Hulk Hogan vying with Vogue editors waiting for the next light, it would be better to give pedestrians a little more elbow room."
—*Photograph by Sam Falk/
The New York Times*

Peter Pan, 1905

Eva Le Gallienne played the part, so did Mary Martin and so did Cathy Rigby, among others. But the first production of "Peter Pan" came to the Empire Theater in 1905 with Maude Adams setting the standard for all the Peters to come, starting what one critic called "a nationwide vogue." Ms. Adams played the role until 1918.

—*Photograph from The Museum of the City of New York Theater Collection*

The Little Sparrow, 1950

When Edith Piaf first came to New York in 1947, it was for a show with a dinner intermission at a French bistro. Variety was impressed. "The Gallic chirper waxed as rich as French cooking," it reported. While Louis Armstrong and others were taking their acts to Paris, Maurice Chevalier and Edith Piaf were playing to packed houses here. Her show at the Versailles set a record for the nightclub.

—*Photograph by George Alexanderson/ The New York Times*

Guys and Dolls, 1951

"The oldest established permanent float-
ing crap game in New York" couldn't
have been anywhere but under Times
Square. When it came up for air on the
stage of the Forty-Sixth Street Theater in
November 1950, the Times critic Brooks
Atkinson wrote that it brought "the most
flamboyant population of any show in
town" along with it. "It is a work of art,"
he went on. "It is spontaneous and has
form, style and spirit." The cast included
Stubby Kaye, Isabel Bigley, Sam Levene,
Vivian Blaine and Robert Alda.

—Photograph by Gjon Mili,
LIFE Magazine © Time Inc.

A Raisin in the Sun, 1961

Commenting on Lorraine Hansbury's "A Raisin in the Sun," the Times critic Brooks Atkinson said that "she has told the inner as well as the outer truth about a Negro family in the south side of Chicago." He added, "it is likely to destroy the complacency of any one who sees it." Its star, Sidney Poitier, was, in the critic's opinion, "remarkable, with a power that is always under control." Poitier's co-stars Ruby Dee and Diana Sands, the review went on, "bring variety and excitement to a first-rate performance."

—Photograph by Friedman-Abeles/ The Billy Rose Theatre Collection, The New York Public Library for the Performing Arts

A Streetcar Named Desire, 1947

When Tennessee Williams's "Streetcar Named Desire" opened at the Barrymore Theater in 1947, the Times critic Brooks Atkinson wrote that "the acting and play-writing are perfectly blended," with the work of Jessica Tandy as Blanche DuBois, being "superb." The acting of Marlon Brando as Stanley Kowalski was "high quality indeed," Atkinson wrote.

—Photograph by Eileen Darby ©

On the Town, 1944

The musical "On the Town" came from the mind of Jerome Robbins, inspired by his ballet "Fancy Free." With a book by Betty Comden and Adolph Green and music by Leonard Bernstein, it came to Broadway with a wonderful pedigree. In the dancer Sono Osato, Robbins found a perfect dancer and interpreter of his ideas for his first Broadway show. The Times critic Lewis Nichols wrote that "Miss Osato brought down the highest rafters when she appeared a year ago in 'One Touch of Venus,' and there is no reason to replace any of those rafters now."
—*Photograph by Eileen Darby ©*

The Mouse That Roared, 1996

The Times Square renaissance began in earnest in 1995 when the Walt Disney Company started its restoration of the New Amsterdam Theater on 42nd Street. Not long afterward the company opened one of its Disney stores right next door with a figure of Mickey Mouse standing on the marquee. In 1935, two years before the New Amsterdam was turned into a movie theater, Mickey starred in his first color picture, "The Band Concert," and nobody, least of all Walt Disney himself, would have believed that Mickey Mouse would become the unofficial Mayor of Times Square.
—*Photograph by Nancy Siesel/The New York Times*

South Pacific, 1951

When Rodgers and Hammerstein's "South Pacific" arrived on Broadway in 1949, everyone agreed that Mary Martin's portrayal of Ensign Nellie Forbush was going to be a tough act to follow. But Ms. Martin eventually moved on, and the show went on with Martha Wright seamlessly moving into the role. It went on and on and on, in fact, until it reached 1,925 performances.
—Photograph by Alfredo Valente

Nightclubbing, 1930's

When Prohibition shut down hotel grills and roof gardens and sent fancy restaurants into limbo, there was no place to go dancing except a speakeasy, where the drinks were appalling and the prices outrageous. In the mid 1920's, the press agent Nils T. Granlund re-invented the nightclub, and with it a minimum charge that would help meet expenses in the same way the old cover charge did. His place on Broadway between 48th and 49th Streets, which he called the Hollywood Restaurant, featured big bands, big stars and beautiful women (Alice Faye started her career as a dancer there), but no liquor. If you brought your own, they'd sell you a set-up, usually a glass of ginger ale, for a dollar. It was an idea whose time had come, and within a year, nightclubs were everywhere. The best of them were in Times Square, including the China Doll, Billy Rose's Diamond Horseshoe, the Latin Quarter and the Versailles, along with the Paradise, another Granlund club, where this shimmy dancer gave the customers their minimum's worth.
—Photograph by Remie Lohse/ Archive Photos

Blur of Excitement, 1995

According to the Times Square Business Improvement District, which is supported by property owners and businesses in the area to provide amenities for the millions of people who live, work and visit the Crossroads of the World, as much as $4 billion has already been invested to create the "new" Times Square. Among other numbers from the BID: 399 property owners, not counting residential condos and co-ops; some 1,500 businesses and organizations, from Viacom/MTV to Morgan Stanley; 21 million square feet of office space and 2.4 million more being built; one-fifth of all New York City hotel rooms — 12,500 now in the neighborhood with another 3,000 on the way; 3.9 million overnight visitors each year, and 26 million day-trippers; 11.5 million tickets sold for Broadway shows in the 1997- 98 season, 1.5 million of them at the Theater Development Fund's discount TKTS booth; more than 251 restaurants, 10 movie theaters and 22 landmarked Broadway theaters. And believe it or not, nearly 27,000 people actually live in the Times Square area, equal to the population of Eureka, Calif.; about 231,000 folks go to work there every day.

—Photograph by Chang W. Lee/
The New York Times

HIGH TIMES, TOUGH TIMES

High Times, Tough Times

Entering Into Society, 1964

Before the Astor Hotel was demolished in 1968, it was a center of New York's social scene. Among its annual events was the Debutante Ball, where young women were properly introduced into society. Tradition kept them out of sight before the big event, during which time they were trained in the social graces. During this period they were called "rosebuds," anticipating the night they would come into full flower in the Astor Ballroom. The receiving line was the high point of the affair, and women who had been there before carefully coached the newly minted ladies on how to behave.

—*Photograph by Larry C. Morris/*
The New York Times

On the Street, 1976
(Overleaf)

Among the fixtures that have almost disappeared from the "new" Times Square are the massage parlors that were cheek by jowl, especially along Eighth Avenue. In the 1940's, when Eighth Avenue was about as seamy as any street in town, most of the action was hidden in brothels, where women lived and worked every day but Sunday. On Monday mornings they could be seen all over Times Square carrying hatboxes containing clean clothes they might need before their next day off. Their choice of luggage was intended to make them appear to be runway models.

—*Photograph by Jack Manning/*
The New York Times

Most cities have a right side and wrong side. One is respectable, the other seamy. Somehow, Times Square is both. It is the place where dime-a-dance partners in old-fashioned dance halls have rubbed elbows with debutantes on the way to trendy new restaurants, where executives have found escape in Shakespeare and in shimmy dancers. A philosopher would say that Times Square is about choice. Good? Bad? Here, no one's indifferent.

At the end of the 19th century, saloons and dance halls were New York's No. 1 tourist attraction, but as the city surged northward, the gentry glided into the area in the West 20's that had been the city's center of sin. The gamblers and the con men, the prostitutes and the pickpockets moved north, as well — to Times Square. When the theater district, elegant hotels and pricey restaurants followed, they stood their ground: Times Square was big enough for everybody. The neighborhood became a unique combination of the best and worst, all squeezed together in a few garish square blocks.

The "new" Times Square, with its family-friendly attractions, hasn't completely changed the mix; it remains a tourist mecca, though for different reasons than the old Times Square was. But it is still a place of improbable contrasts. Old-timers miss the honky-tonk flavor, the beer-and-cigarette smell drifting out of the bars. Yet Times Square is no suburban mall. Out-of-towners know they're not in Kansas any more when they walk these streets.

The
MOTION PICTURE
SHOWING
IN THIS THEATER
ARE ONLY
FOR MATURE
ADULTS OVER
21 WHO ARE
NOT EASILY
OFFENDED

It's a Raid, 1971

Even though it posted a warning to its patrons that they had to be mature and thick-skinned, the management of the Avon Theater on 42nd Street neglected to point out that they might be arrested for buying a ticket, as happened to these theatergoers.

—*Photograph by Neal Boenzi/ The New York Times*

Nickelodeon, 1960

Before Times Square arcades began offering higher-priced "previews" of stag movies in coin-operated videotape machines, a guy could watch grainy "midget movies" of strippers for a nickel. The term referred to the length of the film loops, which were so short a patron of the art form had to be careful not to blink.

—*Photograph by John C. Orris/ The New York Times*

Can You Spare a Dime?, 1965
The terms are many — beggars, bums, panhandlers, bag ladies. Call them what you will, Times Square has known more than its share of those in need. It is a logical place to congregate because the square has many potential donors for the down and out. And over the years, help for the helpless has also been available there.
—*Photograph by Larry C. Morris/*
The New York Times

The Mother of the Queen, 1954
Common wisdom has it that if you stand in Times Square for an hour or so, you will see someone you know or who knows someone you know. There is also a chance that you'll see a movie star or even a queen, as was the case the night Queen Elizabeth, the mother of England's Elizabeth II, brought greetings from the Court of St. James's to the premiere of "The Pajama Game" at the St. James Theater.
—*Photograph by Larry C. Morris/*
The New York Times

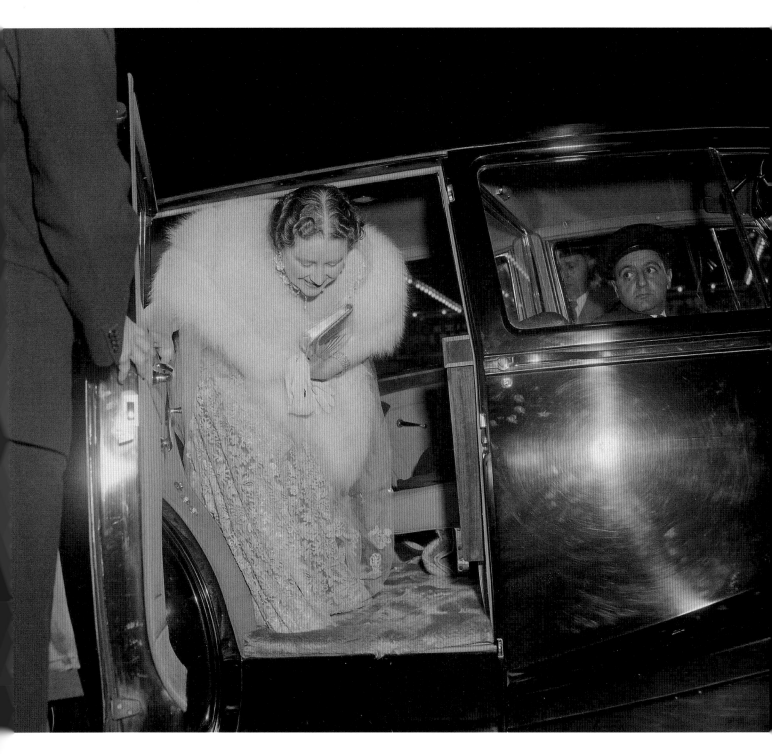

Happy Hour, circa 1900
The Old-Time Barroom, a Times Square hangout that became one of the victims of Prohibition, along with a host of tonier places, had a back room where the regulars gathered and where a stranger might get the bum's rush or worse.
—*Photograph by Brown Brothers*

Playing Dress-Up, 1936
Among the most eagerly anticipated events at the Astor Hotel was the Beaux-Arts Ball, for which revelers appeared in costume. The highlight of the proceedings was a grand pageant that gave all the dancers a chance to show off their creativity, after which they glided onto the ballroom's dance floor.
—*Photographer Unknown*

The Harem, 1972

The notice that this establishment is "unlicensed" differentiates it from professional masseuses, who were. Storefronts such as this were left open because they claimed to sell only body rubs. But in practice, many also sold sex, and were the subject of occasional morals sweeps, often around election time.
—*Photograph by Eddie Hausner/ The New York Times*

Gotta Dance, 1948

Businessmen and out-of-town visitors could enjoy female companionship and a bit of dancing for a dime back in the 30's and 40's at halls like the Orpheum Dance Palace. The women were known as "taxi dancers" because their fee of ten cents a dance was similar to the charge on a taxi meter. Like cabbies, they also expected tips. Making dates with dancers was strictly forbidden in most dance halls, but it was a rule frequently broken.
—*Photograph by Sam Falk/ The New York Times*

Sex Signs Off, 1997
One of Times Square's oldest sex-oriented movies theaters, Eros, finally fell to the inevitable as the neighborhood changed. Back in the 1950's when movies were still squeaky clean, the only place to find sex on film was in an "art house" that showed foreign movies. The longest-running of those in Times Square was the World Theater on 49th Street.
—*Photograph by Chang W. Lee/ The New York Times*

Burlesque's Comeback, 1966
Burlesque was pronounced dead more than 30 years before, but in the 1960's strippers began reappearing in what were known as topless clubs. Like the old burlesque theaters, the very name offended many and owners responded by changing it to "stopless."
—*Photograph by Sam Falk/The New York Times*

THE NAMESAKE

The Namesake

In 1851, when The New York Times published "Vol. 1…No. 1," Manhattan above 42nd Street was countryside dotted with farms and villages. The heart of New York in those days was far downtown; even City Hall was considered the boondocks. But City Hall (and Mayor Ambrose Kingsland and his band of aldermen) needed watching, so the paper's founder, Henry Raymond, rented office space nearby on Nassau Street. There were other considerations, too. The seaport, the only source of news from Europe, was a short walk from Raymond's new newsroom. The theater district was just around the corner, and anybody who mattered lived and worked nearby. The city had a hyphen in its name (New-York) and The New-York Times had a period after its. The Times flourished, then floundered. In 1871, it exposed the corruption of William Marcy (Boss) Tweed and ended Tammany Hall's chokehold on New York politics. But by 1896, The Times's circulation had sunk to 9,000. Enter Adolph S. Ochs, a onetime printer's apprentice who had become the publisher of The Chattanooga Times in Tennessee. He bought The New York Times for $75,000 at a court-run bankruptcy auction. He started using the motto "All the New That's Fit to Print" and promised to give the news "impartially, without fear or favor."

Everybody laughed, especially Ochs's competitors, when he announced in 1902 a plan to move The Times uptown to 42nd Street. Sure, theaters had begun creeping into Long Acre Square (as Times Square was then known) and work had begun on the New York Public Library two blocks to the east. But people couldn't help but ask how the paper was going to cover the action so far downtown. Ochs was betting on the new subway to carry reporters (and freshly-printed papers) faster than any horse-drawn wagon. He was also betting on leased telegraph lines and even the "long distance" telephone, which had just been introduced with the laying of a cable between New York and Newark.

The hyphen disappeared in the 1890's; the period lasted until the 1960's, long after New York City gave the square The Times's name. Ochs's vision of the area was confirmed when he proudly ran a story on April 9, 1904, under the headline, "Times Square is the Name of the City's New Centre."

Onward and Upward, 1903–4

The first issue of The New York Times was published in an unfinished office building at 113 Nassau Street on Sept. 18, 1851. Three years later the paper moved to bigger quarters in a brownstone at Beekman and Nassau Streets and in less than three more years it built its own five-story building on Park Row overlooking City Hall. In 1902, the paper's relatively new owner, Adolph S. Ochs, bought a parcel of land on 42nd Street between Broadway and Seventh Avenue. By the following summer, work was under way on what was billed as "the deepest hole in town" to accommodate The Times's presses, under the IRT subway station that was being built at the same time. The steel skeleton rose floor by floor followed by cladding in brick, terra cotta and limestone. The 25-story tower was designed by the architects C.L.W. Eidlitz and Andrew McKenzie as a modern version of Giotto's tower in Florence. When the building was finished in 1904 it was, at 375 feet, the second-tallest building in the world, after the 386-foot Park Row Building. But considering that its pressroom was 55 feet below the street, its overall height top to bottom was the greatest anyone had ever seen.

—*Photographs by The New York Times*

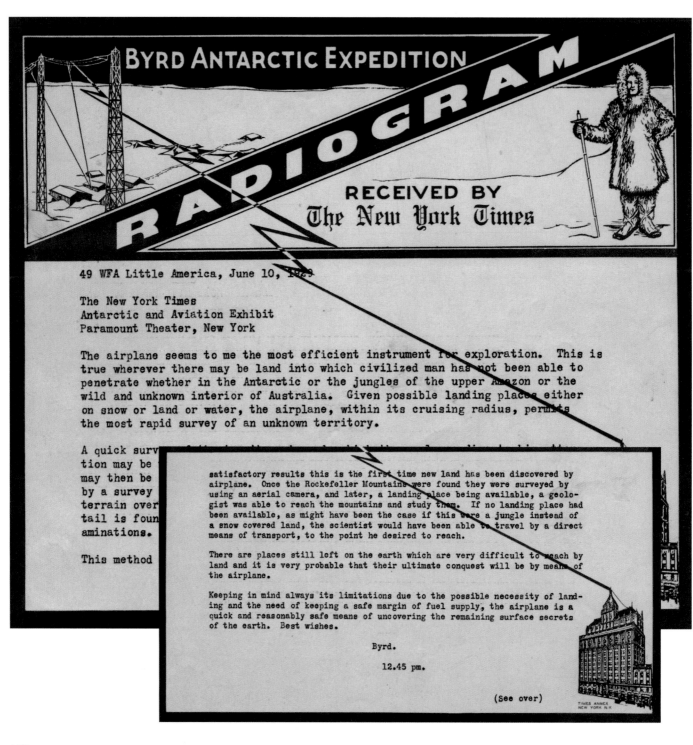

BYRD ANTARCTIC EXPEDITION

RADIOGRAM

RECEIVED BY
The New York Times

49 WFA Little America, June 10, 1929

The New York Times
Antarctic and Aviation Exhibit
Paramount Theater, New York

The airplane seems to me the most efficient instrument for exploration. This is
true wherever there may be land into which civilized man has not been able to
penetrate whether in the Antarctic or the jungles of the upper Amazon or the
wild and unknown interior of Australia. Given possible landing places either
on snow or land or water, the airplane, within its cruising radius, permits
the most rapid survey of an unknown territory.

A quick surv... [of this territory?] ...
tion may be ...
may then be ...
by a survey ...
terrain over ...
tail is foun... ...
aminations. ...

This method ...

satisfactory results this is the first time new land has been discovered by
airplane. Once the Rockefeller Mountains were found they were surveyed by
using an aerial camera, and later, a landing place being available, a geolo-
gist was able to reach the mountains and study them. If no landing place had
been available, as might have been the case if this were a jungle instead of
a snow covered land, the scientist would have been able to travel by a direct
means of transport, to the point he desired to reach.

There are places still left on the earth which are very difficult to reach by
land and it is very probable that their ultimate conquest will be by means of
the airplane.

Keeping in mind always its limitations due to the possible necessity of landing and the need of keeping a safe margin of fuel supply, the airplane is a
quick and reasonably safe means of uncovering the remaining surface secrets
of the earth. Best wishes.

Byrd.

12.45 pm.

(See over)

TIMES ANNEX
NEW YORK N.Y.

The World Beyond the Square

A few months before The Times moved uptown, Carr Van Anda became its managing editor. Both he and the publisher, Adolph S. Ochs, had a natural curiosity for news about science, aviation and exploration and in 1907, they helped finance Marconi's new wireless to gather news faster from farther away. Their practice of contributing funds for broadening mankind's horizons allowed them to publish Robert E. Peary's personal account of the discovery of the North Pole in 1909. The following year, Van Anda hired a special train to follow Glenn Curtiss on his pioneering flight from Albany to New York and scooped The New York World, which had given Curtiss a $10,000 prize for the accomplishment. It was also Van Anda who pieced together bits of information and came up with an exclusive first account on the sinking of the Titanic in 1912. The tradition continued with a first-person report by Comdr. Richard E. Byrd as he became the first man to fly over the South Pole in 1929.

—*Photographer Unknown*

State of the Newsgathering Art, 1945

The Times newsroom on 43rd Street is filled with computer terminals, fax machines and other symbols of modern communications, but back in 1945, when "cut and paste" meant using scissors and a jar of glue, it was a much different, and noisier, place. Editors worked with articles typed on manual typewriters or received through clattering teletype machines. The copy was later hand-carried to the floor above, where it was set in type on huge linotype machines — all within tight deadlines. Most of that work is now handled electronically. Another obvious change over the 50-plus years is that many more jobs are occupied by women and an ethnic mix that better reflects the communities The Times serves. Back in '45, even the top editors' secretaries were white men. —*Photograph by The New York Times*

Text visible in the photograph:

READ, THE EYEWITNESS STORY of the
ATOMIC BOMB
By WILLIAM L. LAURENCE
who prepared the Army press releases and
. . . visited the "MANHATTAN" Plants
. . . studied the bomb's development
. . . witnessed the New Mexico Explosion.
. . . saw the bomb fall on Nagasaki
ARTICLES ARE CURRENTLY APPEARING IN
𝕿𝖍𝖊 𝕹𝖊𝖜 𝖄𝖔𝖗𝖐 𝕿𝖎𝖒𝖊𝖘

"All the News that's Fit to Print."

"All the News that's Fit to Print."

65

The Birth of the Atomic Age, 1945

In early 1945, the United States government asked William L. Laurence, the Pulitzer Prize-winning Times reporter, to write one of the greatest science stories of the 20th century, but he was ordered not to tell anyone about it. He would write the official history of the atom bomb project, code-named "Manhattan" (or the official obituaries, if everyone involved happened to combust in a cataclysmic failure). After the first bomb was dropped on Hiroshima, the government handed The Times the records and on Aug. 7, 1945, Laurence's secrets were finally revealed on the front page. Three days later, Laurence was on an observation plane, the only reporter to see the second atom bomb dropped, this one on Nagasaki. He earned another Pulitzer in 1946 for these firsthand accounts. —*Photograph by Patrick A. Burns/The New York Times*

Get Me Rewrite (undated)
If you call (212) 556-1234, you'll get an automated response from The New York Times asking you to spell out the name of the person you want to reach on your phone's keypad. There are still live operators (along with voice mail), but back when telephones had dials, the switchboard was even more of a nerve center, fielding calls from all over the world and getting them to the right desk without delay.
—*Photograph by The New York Times*

The Paper It's Printed On, 1994
Until 1996, when The Times shut down its presses on 43rd Street, newsprint was delivered by rail from Canada and then carried to 43rd Street by a fleet of flatbed trucks that negotiated Times Square traffic every day. The paper rolls (each weighing close to a ton) were noisily rolled off the trucks into a sub-basement, where they were stored until the presses started running. The paper now prints its New York editions in Edison, N.J., and College Point, Queens.
—*Photograph by Nancy Siesel*

THE LOST CITY

The Lost City

**As Different as Night and Day,
circa 1900 and 1999**
Before The Times came to 42nd Street
and Broadway, the triangular plot was
occupied by the Pabst Hotel, whose
guests had an unobstructed view north to
the spot at 44th Street where Broadway
crosses Seventh Avenue (overleaf). The
view has obviously changed (left). The
ornate white building on the right in the old
photo was Oscar Hammerstein's Olympia
Theater. Among the famous who performed
there were George M. Cohan, Mae West,
Isadora Duncan and the Marx Brothers.
The building was demolished in 1935.

*—Historical photographs:
Photographers unknown*

*—1999 photographs:
Suzanne DeChillo/The New York Times*

Times Square is a work in progress, always has been. Prim turn-of-the-century row houses were torn down for buildings that were more massive and more stylish — Beaux-Arts, perhaps, or wedding-cake Gothic. By midcentury, the demolition crews were at work again, clearing the ground for a new generation of even taller structures. In the 1990's, after still more demolition, work finally began on the long-debated (and long-delayed) redevelopment of Times Square, whose steel and glass raised the rooftops to new heights — an eleventh of a mile, give or take a few feet. One doesn't need bricks and mortar or concrete and cement to give a place like Times Square a fast facelift. Many buildings have been covered with billboards, clocks, bulletin-every-minute moving-message displays, even televisions. But these are not ordinary sets: one outsize monitor contained 560 picture tubes, each about the size of a home TV screen.

Beneath the kaleidoscopic blur of zigzagging headlights, kamikaze bicycle messengers and New Yorkers elbowing their way through life are the mystifying ganglia of the city's infrastructure, largely forgotten but essential: electrical cables next to steam pipes next to water mains next to sewer lines.

And then there is the wonder down under, the 722-mile rapid-transit network that converges on Times Square. The modern-day subway system is simply the old subway system, unified by City Hall in midcentury. August Belmont's Interborough Rapid Transit Company came first, in 1904, and its trains were soon huffing and puffing 24 hours a day. The rapid transitions above ground have not been matched by the rapid transit system below. Sure, the cars are newer and the rails are replaced every few years, but they rumble through the same old tunnels. No wonder some historians credit the IRT's round-the-clock service with bestowing on Times Square, and on New York City itself, a reputation as a place that never closes, never sleeps and never needs to.

Changing Times, 1927 and 1999
The original exterior of the Times Tower was decorated with limestone and terra cotta, and designed to resemble a tower in Florence. In the early 60's, it was stripped to its steel skeleton and its facade clad in marble, which has since been hidden behind advertising signs. The old Times Square lives on in the former Knickerbocker Hotel, whose rooftop decoration still frames this view. Also surviving renovation were the Times Annex (now called the Times Building), in the background at left but blocked from view at right by the skeleton of the new Reuters headquarters, and the Paramount Building, to the right of the old Times Tower.

Broadway and 44th Street, circa 1920 and 1999

John Jacob Astor made his first fortune, in the fur business, in the early 1800's and a second long-lasting one investing heavily in New York real estate. He eventually owned more of Manhattan than any other individual. For $25,000, he bought a former farm, stretching between 42nd and 46th Streets, and from Broadway to the Hudson River, and his heirs turned it into a fashionable neighborhood. In 1909, they anchored their investment with the Astor Hotel, among the most elegant in town. It was demolished in 1968 to make way for One Astor Plaza, the 50-story office tower at first named the J.C. Penney Building. It is now home to Viacom and its offspring, MTV.

Broadway at 42nd Street, 1903 and 1999

Before The Times could build its tower, workers had to
dig a hole for the paper's presses. So down they went,
below the subway that was being built simultaneously.
Today, the former Times Building has disappeared behind
a blanket of signs, and the Condé Nast building has
sprouted across Broadway.

125

Galleries showing premiere exhibitions of
"The Century in Times Square"

Stephen Daiter Gallery, Chicago
Gallery of Contemporary Photography, Santa Monica
Howard Greenberg Gallery, New York
Jackson Fine Art, Atlanta
Robert Koch Gallery, San Francisco

The Newseum, New York

Exhibitions coordinated by photokunst, San Diego